W9-ADX-554

The Harvesters' Vase

Also by Ned O'Gorman

THE NIGHT OF THE HAMMER

ADAM BEFORE HIS MIRROR

THE BUZZARD AND THE PEACOCK

THE HARVESTERS' VASE

VASE

Poems by Ned O'Gorman

MIDDLEBURY COLLEGE
LIBRARY

Harcourt, Brace & World, Inc.
New York

Copyright © 1966, 1967, 1968 by Ned O'Gorman
All rights reserved. No part of this publication
may be reproduced or transmitted in any form
or by any means, electronic or mechanical,
including photocopy, recording, or any
information storage and retrieval system, without
permission in writing from the publisher.
First edition
Library of Congress Catalog Card Number: 68-12589
Printed in the United States of America

Some of the poems in this volume
previously appeared in *The Columbia University
Forum, Jubilee,* and *The Nation.*

To Juliette, Karim, and Jousif
And to the memory of Dorothy Van Ghent

Contents

The Harvesters' Vase

To Bernard the Huntress

For Sister Bernard of Tarrytown

It's the long field that gets you:
the hedges and the fallow edge of the wood;
the moss on the fence at the junction
of the crossbars and the upright posts.
Then the cool wood the hounds hit,
their snouts boiling with foam
to bleed the fox from his hole.

You know how it is, Bernard, when the morning
is not much of a thing but the faint blaze
of willow on the bark of the lawn. From the oak
doors of the Manor you step, dressed in
a black skirt, your hair bunched
at your neck, boots done to a peat shine
that flouts the mare's skin, dull enough to go
like brown gold with the sapphire whip hiding
in the depth of your scarf. And the surge
before the jump when the beast sees the stop
in the field, hauls up its knees, lets fly
its back and you are grafted there, an extolled wing,
that springs exulting from his mane.

Paolo Climbing Down through a Tree
For Paolo Lorimer

He is off to ring the neck of the luncheon
chicken and cut the throat of Sunday's
rabbit. A knife between his teeth
he steps down from the balcony
onto the top branch glowing like
vengeance in the leaves. The roadway
steams. His shadow falls from the branches
breaking up the skin of morning.
I reflect him in my heart, this child
carrying weapons of supper. I carry weapons
too between my teeth, the weapons of will
and music.

        We increase in animality.
The harvest grows in the sun between
the double gates of death and greenery.

The Memorable Thing
about Love

The memorable thing about love is
that it consists of talk rather
more than silence. One of the marks
of lovers is that they must talk
to one another. Christ is, by that
token, the greatest of lovers.

Love too is known by its silence.
It is a mark of a lover's stance
that he is struck dumb before
his beloved. Christ then must be
the finest lover and beloved.

Love is understood by the ways
it discovers to refer all
things to itself, by the sorrow
of its duration, by the
lament in its dearest moments—
in elation, in departure.
So then it must be that Christ
is the most accustomed of lovers.

where I have loved as if
its slag and whips and swagger
on my tongue were sacrament
and sweetness of your face.

The Opal Cycle

1.

In their hands the lovers held the jug of wine
complete to the top. It was a winter night.
The lovers uncontained by ice or polar light
lifted wine up to their mouths and drank. "I
am contained by wine," the cup declared, and
"I," the wine declaimed, "surrounded by the cup
like a continent the fiery center of the globe."
And drained of all compassion but for kisses
they laid the cup between them on the ground
and filled it once again. The brim laps over
and stains the earth between them. The wounds of
arbors cut the glacial surface of the mud.
"It's best to die," the ground laughed loud,
"Olympian to the end, than fret in amplitude
until the skeleton explodes with marrow."
It was the end of the blue cycle of their love.
The opal had begun. The opal cycle is the one
before the last; the last: when love reverts
to fire and the elements. They yawned. The brown
hem of her robe dragged like a vine
of wild, late summer gourds over the frost.

2.

"I loved you," one with eyes color of sand
said to the other, eyes color of cleaved
waters, "before I knew the wild expression
in your hands and could tell the seasons from
the months." The other said: "I loved without
the name of love; without expectation of
love's gifts." On the fields of morning they
stood with backs toward the light in the country of
                              the galaxies.

3.

There were plains there the length of galaxies.
Beyond the farthest but visible point of land,
a distance of about the duration of a thunderclap
a sun began to grow between the earth and the first
heaven. The zodiacal lights, the joining together
of fireballs, soundless weights and balances,
the heaving of the void, the loosening of the cobbles
between the ribs of space, turned by a thin bind
of the wind to yellow, from the outer, tumbling
air, into the center where the sun gathered
like a piled-up grove of forsythia. Each petal
exploded into a fallow heat, the kind that rises
off the fields early in the morning of the hot
                                    harvest months.

4.

The lovers wandered in the raw
worlds' nameless spheres. They
neither touched hands nor
rested to recall their first delights,
for as yet the world was unremembered.
Longitudes and latitudes
of mass and boundaries waited upon
the spirit of the Lord which came
over the edge of the globe, the clays
of its will soldering the rupturing seas
and pinning to the muds the roaring fields.

Toward You I Fall

Toward you I fall though I do not wish to fall.
Toward you I bend my head though I do not wish
to see the light upon your brow. Toward you my
hands reach out. My neck and back seek you in
the dark. I see your body on the wind. It leans
upon my hand and upon the windowpane like frost.
At your waist I watch the moon rise and the lowlands
slide beneath your belly. Waterways mount your breasts.
I snap like green wood. I loose the field.
You bear me off. I lie upon your body where I fall
like a face and plumage on a blooded shield.

Looking Upward at a Waterford Glass Chandelier

For Nora Mathews

When I look upward into that tuned sky
of the glass blower's gut, each baked
drop of running heat brings to me
the time I was a boy and woke to find
the world aslant with wickedness.
I walked into the forest and sat on the bank
of a pool where the springs that lay across
the bottom sent up cold rings of peace.
Trees stood on their tops; in the moss that
clasped the banks, ladybugs and red berries
moved like small horns and pricked the
soundless walls of trees. When the sun
had soared to her flaxen perch and fell
into the pool's cast net, a ripe crack
of yellow feathers tapped the power from
my eyes. Turn now, quickly, to the west
window where the sun has moved over the
brick walls of the vegetable garden and hangs
there to salute this sister sun that pours
out above us in a volley of glass wings.
O dear Nora, hear them, how they greet each other
in this coupling of lights.

The Bathing Place

There it was as if the body
had no origin. As if it came
up from the muds and lingered
here to this perdition.

They stood, sat, knelt and
stretched on a plot of grass
no bigger than a tennis court
seventy naked men in the

match-light of an English sun.
The Cherwell is not a crystal
brook; the currents churn with
weeds and silt but when I punted

past the bathing place a fat man
with graying pubes dove like
a muskrat into the stunted waters.
Four nude boys twisted like slugs

in the sweaty light. A man so old
his skin was matted to his sinew
covered his privates with a woolen
cap. "Why do they come here to this

damp and hidden place. Why do men come
and linger nude when the sun is
hidden in a fetid mist." "They come
for sinister reasons. Not sexual

but natural fantasy draws them bare-
assed to this soggy pitch
where they lie in wait for Sol
to bugger them. He never does."

13

I'd never strip and show my body
to such men who seem so clothed
when they are not. I've lain
naked in the sun but not with men

who look like dry rot in a fallen
tree, who roll on their glue-white
butts snorting at the sun. It takes
style to strip. It's not pulling off

of pants and shirt that makes a body
nude; it's putting on of skin.
I dove once into the Aegean
from a rock on Ios

and brushed against a
jellyfish round as a ten-
gallon hat. That stripped me.
I've not been dressed since.

The Harvesters' Vase
For Sloane Elliott

All things are gods.
                     After having accomplished
the embarkation of the lion there was the
unearthing of the orange sarcophagus and the
polished stone gaming board and its tourmaline
counters. And it could not be but a sign of their
desire that they painted fish upon their corpses'
heads and necks.

                     The entire world for them
was gods.
                     At a harvest festival, fifty men stepped
into a line of march and crossed this black steatite
field on the ripe earth; the wheat shoots were
sharp as crystal on the naked feet of those gleaners
of the Wheat-God's pleasure.
                               The wine pouch flew
from man to man. The sheaves' dried seed fell
and stuck to their brows; their skin pulled tight
across their skulls, for the harvest was hard and
winds curled that summer from the air harrowing
their bodies into craters where they stood all day
collecting the ripe lava of the fields.

                                    When
the temple came in view, cocked on the hill
preened and unconsolable, riot struck the
harvesters in their inner ear. They fell into a
run, belching, clutching at rocks, bleeding,
their bodies bare and black in the sun's mill, and
slammed into the sacred magazines where they upturned
jugs of wine and sacred creams and muted by this

sacral fancy in the steatite thunder of their feast,
they climbed into the precincts of the
Mother Goddess of the Countryside who ran
out of their ears and mouths like a heavy wine.

What Three?

For Maria Schrady

To it they move, as it moves,
from point to point to point
describing in the place they
tread its image, not at any place
complete but where it moves
as three; not at any place
one but where the three are in
the other's path. We know
the trajectory of its life
by the confluence of its planes,
each carried by the other,
each the multiple life of the
other's singular life.
Each the singular habitation
of the other's multiple glory.
These three revel in being
the image of the other's life
though each is without imitation
in the other but is the accurate
self of the inaccurate godhead.
In their motion they reoccur
to each as they pass through
the infinite becoming of their
singular self. And when they
strike out into what they make
and touch the most green
sheaf of their thought, they twist
through space as a vine shunts
through the arbor, gives the globe
to the fruit and returns to the
trellis, and the vineyard breathes
to the triumphant return of the vine.

If He Had Loved Her

If he had loved her
he let no one know.
His friends connived
against him to admit
he numbered her among
his lusts but he would
not let down his guard.
If he loved her
when she lived we knew
nothing then and could
not while she lived demand
a reckoning of her love.
But now our way is clear.
She's dead; he lives on
and when he looks at us
he seems to say: "If you
ask I'll tell you now.
If you move me to recall
her to your private lusts
I'll do it and erect her
in your eyes like a blasted wall."
But dead she is no longer
such a thing to give us pause.
We follow him to the edge
of his street. He had loved
her. He let no one know.
Now when he would tell us all
he knew about her body and her
thought we care for nothing
but this watch we keep
upon his life and say goddam
his memory and his lusts.
Though we thrill to the way
he turns and looks upon us when
we lean out from the doors

and windows as he passes, holding
out his hand, as if she might rise
up from the pavement he walks upon
like a shadow falling from
an overhanging rock.

Plenitude

Where gulls ride
the floating plains
of the sun,
there
is plenitude.
Plenitude
is in the flowers
of the sea,
in the haze at the shell's
edge.
Plenitude salts
divinity
when roots' abundant rods
are heavy
on the earth;
when the lion's mane pulls
down the high grasses.
When the seed rocks
in its cylinder
of privileged
dust
man is proven plenteous
in his courtship.
Beasts are plenitude
of the branch
they slumber on
as the light is in the leaf
it traps.
When the moon
is up,
tides, deprived of harbors
twist their briny necks
to the skies.

A Conversation between Willa Muir, Rudolph Nureyev, and Ned O'Gorman about Excess

Nureyev. How many leaps within the leap?

Willa. Let the end of the thing done
be the leap to the crossed beams of white light.

Nureyev. I shall leap twice into the crossed beams
of white light. Within the rudimentary leap
I shall etch two uncaused fluted turns.

Willa. No. Do not hitch eight horses
to a four-horse carriage.
Two uncaused fluted turns
is eight horses.

Nureyev. Had I no legs, no arms, no
triggered thigh and arch
I'd leap through hoops,
not through crossed
white beams of light
that span the middle of the scene.

Ned. We are grafted to excess.
Beat alphabet get a vine.
Beat vine get a lion.

Willa. Vines and lions are eight horses.

Nureyev. I'll climb vines and ride lions
as the bull-dancers rode their
fancy bulls through Cretan stockyards.

Willa. Excess drains blood of salt and bread.
Edwin cooked excess.
It did not cook him.
It cooks you both.

Nureyev. (Ascending)
I cook space.

Take it and let it sleep among
your friends who grow like emblems
of a dynasty in the rooms of this
great house. Perhaps Stravinsky or Valéry,
Tagore or Mistral, who walked with you through
the aisles of your tropical park, would
think it precise enough to exclaim one
blessing on it. (It will bite the wood
of the cherry table in the tiny drawing room
and settle on the household in one gleaming cleave.)

The room is a blade of vegetable and flower.
The bowl of jasmine mounts the wall
into the white wooden ceiling. A jug of
rosemary catches the jasmine in the spicy yell
of its gentle, fragrant stems and the curtains
made of fine linen with florid scrolls at the edge
blow inward and catch on my bare shoulders.
The axe has gathered the sun
in a nub of blue heat at the center of the field
of slaughter. It pierces to the heavy armor
of my soul. I hear it lift into the air,
hover there and then descend, with the burning glint
of a wing, to free my tongue for this song.

Signs

The world is signaled.
Look. White flags on doorposts,
red flags on barns
and in the tavern a tin cup
chained like a bible
to the table.
O tin cup, bits of cloth,
boots that charge
between the doorposts
to hoot of
wars and harvests . . .

These stop the traveler.
He sees the white flag.
A dead child?
A marriage sheet?
Pestilence within?

The white flag hangs to say,
"The bread is done."
"New bread within."
The housewife broods above
the table. The new loaf
stands before her, a crusty,
steamy temple making brown
advances on the walls and floor.
Heat rises from the
open oven door.
(White flour on the
underside of new bread
is dry and pure.)
Mice slide across the empty
flour bin.

The red flag hangs to say,
"The calf is dead." His belly
open and his bulk strung up
in the slaughterhouse.
Blood from the neck
slides like dew
off the shiny hoof.
O severed head of calf
skinned to crystal
nerve. How your muzzle
hairy and wet shines
on the butcher's marble counter.
O the leg, the neck,
the glad, dumb mouth, the small
curved beginning of
a horn . . .

Go watch it dwindle
into meat and buy it for
your table.
The flags are signs
of commerce
and bid gold and silver come
to hallow them.

The chained cup says,
"Drink but do not steal the thing."
The crock beside the cup is
full. The wooden funnel
hanging by the cask
is wet with gin.

O smell of garlic
in the palm.

O sea urchin
and the live crab within
the husk.

O stink of iodine.
O black seaweed and salty syrup
of the sands on
the umber spikes.

O bowl of jasmine.
O jugs of rosemary.

A herdsman, spurs about his boots
like silver thorns,
a soldier with his breath
cut short
charge between the doorposts,
gouge out their mark
upon the table
and shout,
"All life is blest."
"There is new grain in the bin."
"Juniper berries ferment in the barrels."
"Ovens swell with fire."
"The calf slides his neck along the axe."

And
alamos, erect as sprays of
wind, breathed upon the night
as the dry funnel hissed
for gin and the chained cup rose
like frost
to the herdsman's salty lips.

The Galilean Light
For Molly Finn

St. Peter's Fish, the flat hot bread,
the wheat within the tow of the sun,
the light upon the fin, the crust,
the stem of food, O Molly, lizards
move like clocks across the stones:
silence falls upon the surface
of the sea, dissolves like bread
upon the white fish's eyes in Galilee
where Jesus brushed the pollen from his beard.
A bird flew up from a rocky field,
brown wings, marks of leaves upon his feathers;
it seemed if Christ had scared it up returning home
from drinking minted tea. Goat, flower, fox,
lamb, river bed, field, moon and borderland,
in the rough tissue of Galilean light
where the bees from Tabor gather in their glee
when hives are filled with honey,
the sleep of flowers on their wings,
fall in shadows blue and green as rain upon this land
and sea where Jesus took the air in Galilee.

The Paralytic

I have waited now ten years
to hear this pool speak through my tears.
Legs bent under me,
my neck a hangman's noose. I cannot see
but what the inside of my eyes' watch
of the brain's flood. I am a golden face
beneath an iron mask. There is a case
to be made for me: ten years on this
pallet; each time the angel hissed
through the surface some rich man
knocked me over and stepped, rotten in the can,
puce lipped, into the green water
and stepped out pure as any rabbi's virgin daughter.
I stay a wreck on the water's edge;
nose running, face agape and no pledge
from the priest to move me up one place
closer to the edge. That bastard takes money for the race
into the pool—a change of pallet to the right
or left—and when the angel coughs upon the light
he who was quickest with the gold falls
splashing to his cure. I'll jump the gun some day,
swallow the burly pollen of the pool and rise up
like a fern from moss, lithe, reposed, floating, erect and cool.

Hands

Never was such a portent as this love,
even as prophets dream, so impossible
to reckon. There was space and then
no space was but the vine of our hands
clasped together tight as the press about
the blazing grape. Raw salts, muds of herbs
and fossil, germs of ore, steamed from the
black yeast of the earth. When your
fingers pressed upon my eyes, muscle and
vein wheeled between us in a small typhoon.
We brought our wrists to the other's lips
and fell asleep like two sounds on the risen
bank of a coral reef, as saffron fish nets
swung on their poles toward the sea.

To X Who Never Existed
Except in Reality

The wilderness I brought her I brought
in arms that sang like sheaves of wind
to lie across her face. I leaned into the
steamy target of her soul, took my place
above her and descended down like the
mariner who follows the phosphorescent tides
all night and comes at dawn upon the perfumed
sun resting on a dolphin's foamy back.
And when we reached the randy climate
of repose I lay upon her in the delivered
glory of our flesh as if I never knew but
hours at her lips and days above her
turning like a windmill to lift up the first
spume of water toward the infertile sun.

Haircutting

"Come, untrimmed path, and sit upon that stool."
She unfolds a sheet and covers him from head
to toe. Between the left ear and the skull
she lops. No hound chasing frogs into a hornets'
nest came out less chewed than he, Luis,
who looks into a triptych mirror and concedes
that art had lost the day to fancy and his wife's
economies. A thousand spiders scud across
the floor. A scar atop the ear, a neck too bald
for tact, the forelock gone, the crown indented
like a saw. "Once," he said, "a Corsair and his
mount assumed the enemy asleep but met him
armed with candor and a knife upon
the lunar battlements of an incompleted strategy."

At the Tomb of Ha'ari

In the Galilean zone of the heavy Eastern sun,
the lion whelps gather at the blue grave to pick
his brain.

The light holds down the four corners of the earth.

The lion whelps rend their cloaks and fall muttering
in the dust.

"Izhak Luria, Rabbi, The Lion, who called up the seven
shepherds of Israel to read the Torah on the Sabbath,
leap now from the eclipse of light you kept in a band
around your hat, creep from this blue box and tell us
the forms-of-what-is-not."

"Schicinna," he had said, "is the eking out of Jehovah's
beard through the world." He said it, standing on his
right to say it, upon the pavement of the thresher's floor
when the wheat had been spilt through the stone mill
like blood.

From nowhere came sound: the cracking of muds, the jingle
of bells, the bellying forth of a pomegranate, the fall
of stones through water. A field of wheat sprang from the
rocks beneath him.

The valley crept on all fours into the synagogue. Ha'ari
unrolled the light around his hat and found on the edge of
the scroll, the waters of life and a fish swimming in them—
dorsal fin white as sandstone and petal of a daisy. It
slid against the text that was linked in the Rabbi's
dream-of-what-was-not-but-was-to-come, to the flesh of
the sun.

A hag with yellow braided hair who kept the keys squinted
at the lion in the shadow of the screen in the women's
gallery. When he lifted up his eyes to call the presences
not there but possible, the walls of the room screamed, the
air leapt for joy. Grapes fell from the thick arbor
on the roof. The seven-branched candelabra broke like
an arrow, split on the edge of a comet, into flame.

The woman in the gallery fell to the thresher's floor.
She lay at his feet in the whispering muds, the pomegranate
and wheat bright as ikon paints in the synagogue's
eternal dusk. She undid her hair and laid the Rabbi
out like the rule of life upon the pavement. He opened
his eyes and the Queen of Storm and Harvest set her foot
upon his brow. He rent his cloak and breathed in the
ghost-of-what-was-not.

The lion whelps in broad-brimmed, ermine hats, carried
him to the hillside and put him to rest in a blue stone box.

Until now, each year, on the day he died, the whelps come
and howl into their beards. The air near the tomb is
heavy with the sounds of the waters of life, herbs and the
dry light of the interior of the ark. Behind the
screen in the women's gallery a hag with yellow braids
watches the door, the blue grave and the eyes of the
lion whelps for the return of the lion and the
forms-of-those-things-that-yet-are-not-but-are-to-come.

The Donkey

The Donkey who is in the field
in this increasing fall is
tall as a hedge of wild rose.
He seals our dreams with grace:
a deliverance from rage
and intolerance of animals.
He is the gift of fallen apples
and rows of corn and ravens.
The dumb hoof of our blood
heaves on the barbed green.
He trots upon the sun. The horizon
brays through the orchard. His eyes
have seen the frost but
he burns with spring and Cici's hands
like links of crocus around his neck.

On the Splendor of Signs

The Intruder bears upon his arms shields
carved with the shapes of the whorls on shells.
In his hands he carries a square cage.
The bells hung within it and the small
flowers fixed in the corners give it an air
of a field. He rises into the riggings
seething like an alphabet. Standing
in the dark below my thoughts he has the
shape of the hull of this ship seen from
underwater. My hand presses into the tiller;
the wind freezes the mainsail. I see the
fixed throw of his arm and the blast of clouds
at his finger tips when I lift my hands, when the
keel forced the salt to my eyes, to his lips.

The Fortress

The river floats below it
without armor. I walk on
the ramparts that click
in the black stubble of
the snow. I am cast there
like rubble from the fit
of a violent machine.
The flag on the watchtower
and the spiked gate hold
judgment on the sky. Guns
nest in the hill beyond
where the moon catches up
the polish on the butts.
I am the night and wait to
contain the fortress in my
brow as a toad clasps
the emerald in its swamp-weed stare.

of a deck. A flower tumbles down
the empty street stem over bud.
A white mare's head is pinned
by a spoke in the mud.

The soldier who guards the river bend
falls into a dream of house and wife.
Boy child and woman sitting on a stone wall
bordering one edge of a courtyard.

As he dreamed, the enemy, left to guard the walls
of a ruined fort, looked up from his trumpet
and saw the white plume of the dreaming guard
swagger in a down current of sun and wind.

He moves upon him with a short knife,
pulls it down through the plume and eye,
and plunges it into his throat.

In his dream the knife struck the brain
as the child prepared to jump from wall to
cobble pavement. Precisely it cut the retina in two
when his white sandal touched the cobble,
when his toe brushed the first rounded
sunlit curve of the pavement.

He swallows in the light and spits it out again.

The scene: the ruined altar. The
door of the ark bent on its silver
hinges. Flies on the holy breads.
A woman hit by the descent of the Rose Window
is impaled on the altar rail.

The wife lays the table
in the shade of the well,
in the center of the courtyard:

cool butter
cream on berries
red melon
on the white plate.

The Death of the King

It was a day out of season.
Tides rushed up to the cliffs
where children had danced on the
witching rocks in the early
hot hours. The river that
ought to have frozen stiff
seeped into the sleigh carrying
the king into the city. The
fences on the west hill pushed
against the dry fields and a
blood-red hex spawned on
the stones at the base of the temple.
Women dropped the outer veil
from their faces and men walked
in the shadows. Flowers that
ought not have bloomed flourished
in the fields where the king
walked with his sharp-eyed thugs.
At the rise of the hill
where the winds tunnel into the sun
a black rain hit the span
of the golden parasol; scepter
and jeweled glove went under the
earth and slaughtering waters
hooked the brain of the king out.
I picked up fire and crested glass
and walked out of season. I could not
hear my thoughts so great the wildness
of the wild beasts; so hard the stones
that rang at my footfall, on the sunless hillsides.

2. THE PREPARATION OF THE BODY

O the head. Watch how it is placed.
Undo the studded collar; wind cloths

around the wound at the base of the skull.
Unclench the jaw. O
how the blood has gone through the neck and
see, there is a blank heat in the eyes.
Pest death comes
from the top of the head,
to the nose,
onto the breastbone,
to the belly,
nicking the loins,
toppling over the groin,
to the knees where it slides
to the feet like a clipper ship
furling its sails.
Death cracks over the muffled drums;
and over the body, the light, like a white-hot coin,
presses down upon his brow
as it hovers on the frosty transformation into stone.

3. THE PROCESSION TO THE TOMB

The black stallion pulled the crowd through the dark bells.

The coffin jogged on the mind,
that jogged on the caisson,
that jogged on the earth,
as this new birth of death clopped along the roadway,
slow as the final, salty lurch of the landed trout.

To be dead.
To be dead.

The procession bore down into the turf.
The caisson creaked over the rocks
and the glistering shields of black enamels
held by the thugs with the eyes of lapis
pressed back the mob that barked like hounds
on the lolling, blood-pulled light.

The body within touched the silver roof
with each drop of the cannon mouth,
with each golden thud of the weighted, painted hoofs.

4. THE BURIAL

It took three men with
dynamite and a pulley
to lift the stone from the
side of the hill at the
sunless fall.
The place was far from the village
and the wagon broke when the stone
was laid upon it. It took two
wagons, the rock's weight
resting part on one, part on the other,
to deliver it to the cave.
The opening in the rock was crowded
with shadows. One man cleared away the
weeds. Tipped slightly
to the left the king was carried in
and set upon a stone table carved into the wall.
The followers of the cart
stood on the verge of the closing cave.
A slab of wood was cut
from under two gutters of sand
that let down the door,
striking sparks from the rocky loam.
Within dark settled
and the last light careened from wall to wall
seeking space, flashed in agony
and turned to silt.
When the darkness rusted into dawn the lean
stone shined as if a mind had forced it with its eyes.

Goggling on the Red Sea

Hot day, hot night. A screen of waters, lizard
green stuck to my face. My senses were a
smoky heap. Thought died on a crack. Flat night.
Flies. The world crowed
                                        when an ice-bearing
highland sliding through the sea brought me
on my belly to the peak of a coral reef. Parrot
fish and black, spiny urchin, in the Red Sea
River, on a band of liquid bone, joined in a battle
of paints. How blessed it was, sucked to the bowed
running curve of the reef where water, fish, color
enjambed and beaten led me through prisms of stone
into the shark's blunt shadow.

                                        The highland
passed over me, scraping on the dusky air
where half my body caught like a wire on the
clotting light. I floated on and night,
a great squid, reached down tentacle over
tentacle into the reef and turned the undersea
and all the beasts into a slaty mist.

                                        The
cantoring sun beached on the sandstone hills.
I floated on the Red Sea's salty blood.
On floors of limestone, I hooked the flood.

Obsession

The honeycomb slips between my eyes
and lallygaggles there smelling like
the curd of sugar fields afire.
I fall in a sticky faint.
Honey in pots or driven onto crusts
of bread derange my tongue. Buzz buzz buzz.
I will stick to my center of sour herbs
or go hexagon.

The Surfer

There was smoke and fire in the hills
when the surfer walked to the shore.
He held the board above him,
balancing it like a tusk in the dawn.
He slipped into the foam of the heavy sea.
The water met the pelt of sand:
each separate as the beginning and end
of a drumbeat. The board rose
like a bud to bless him. The light
gleamed in the oil of the rising sun.
He lay on his belly and drove his arms into
the sea and plowed his way to the acre
where the big wave bred. He edged
toward the crest, climbed it and when he
reached the top, a bird of clawed and feathered salt,
he strode on trident legs over terraces of shells
and demented fish, swooped through the chiming foam
to the sand where the elements, hungry princes
snarling and whining on the hairbreadth
of their borders, descended toward him.

The Spasm before the Last

The spasm before the last convulsed him
to the bone. The shelf of china jogged
one hair closer to the edge. He felt
the rug go tight. The window frame
pulled a crack away from the wall.
"O Lord if this be the end of time,
protect at least those Dresden pots,
that your angels might discover
color amid the ashes' triumphant piles."
He knew he had not known anything
as beauteous as those pots. Life had
been like that: a jog to the end of a shelf.
First the waterfalls and crops, then marriages,
children, the death of friends, marriages again.
One day he bent over the herbs on the garden's
shaded border and smelt the end.
                                        He heard
his wife walk up the stair: "The garden's in
tumult: a lark sits on the ivy wall."
The final tremor came. The Dresden pots
shattered on the floor. His hands were severed
from his wrists, his head collapsed in ashes. The ivy
and the lark went up in a green smoke.

The Eden of the Vegetables

I am apple. You are pear.
They are weeds. Those, herbs.
The others, beans of various sorts.
Around the corner, the crowd:
cucumbers, onions, tiger lilies,
radishes and wild garlic. The rabble,
above the lawn on the stone terrace:
berries, asparagus, dandelions and
morning glories. We hang on our branches,
you Lady Pear, I Sir Apple. The world
rests, a cabbage too large for eating,
in the garden of days. The worm, beetle
and slug hover about, hissing and slicing
away at sap. The grass watches.
In the distance the sound of metal drives
through the loam and aloft in the toting
shadows: pruning sticks, torches, ladders, and the jam pot.